LIFE WITH JUVENILE IDIOPATHIC ARTHRITIS

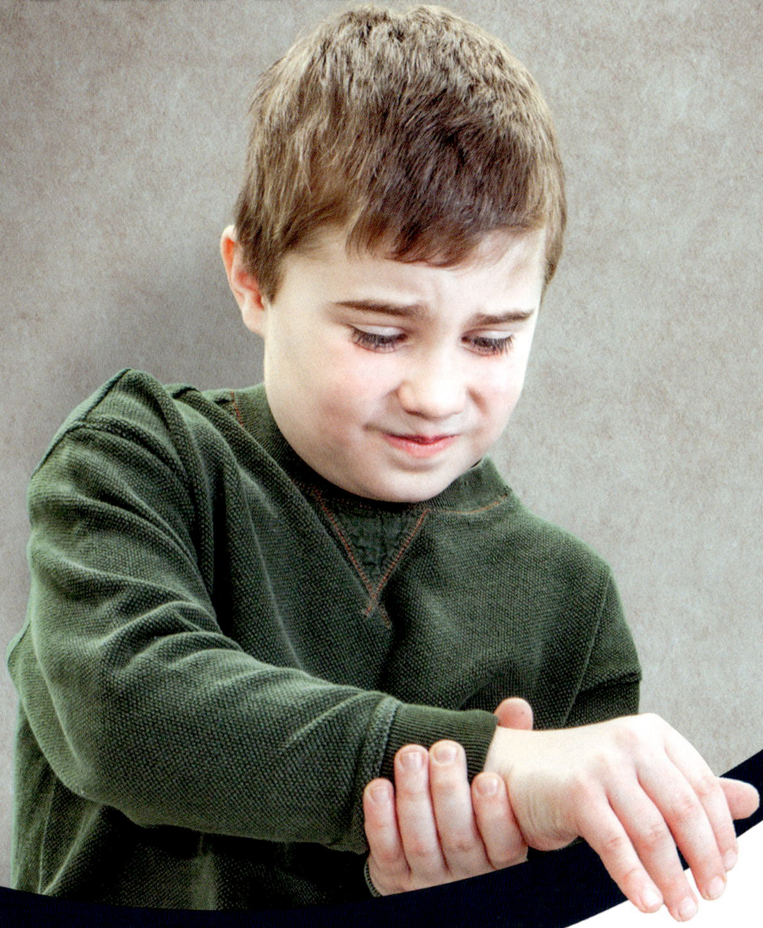

BY JAMES BOW

The Child's World®
childsworld.com

Published by The Child's World®
1980 Lookout Drive • Mankato, MN 56003-1705
800-599-READ • www.childsworld.com

Content Consultant: Daniel Lovell, M.D., Professor of Pediatrics, University of Cincinnati School of Medicine

Photographs ©: Bronwyn Photo/Shutterstock Images, cover, 1; Shutterstock Images, 5, 10; Wave Break Media/Shutterstock Images, 6; iStockphoto, 9, 12, 18, 20; Julio Cortez/AP Images, 14; Lucy Nicholson/Reuters/Newscom, 17

ISBN 9781503825147
LCCN 2017959683

Printed in the United States of America
PA02375

TABLE OF CONTENTS

FAST FACTS

- Juvenile idiopathic arthritis (JIA) is an autoimmune disease. This type of disease occurs when a body's **immune system** attacks healthy cells and tissues, causing **inflammation**, stiffness, and pain.
- JIA can start off with joint pain and extreme tiredness, similar to the flu. These symptoms sometimes fade or lessen, and the joint swelling may not develop for some time. This makes JIA hard to **diagnose**.
- JIA makes physical activity painful. Children with JIA may not have the energy to play or focus on school. JIA affects more than 50,000 U.S. children.
- Scientists aren't sure what causes JIA. Some think it might be caused by a problem in a person's **genes**. Others think it may be caused by a **virus**.
- There is no cure for JIA, but doctors are searching for one. Medicines and exercises can control the disease and reduce the pain. Medicines come in the form of pills or shots. These treatments can help minimize or avoid joint damage.

JIA AND INFLAMMATION

Joints are parts of the body where two bones meet. JIA can affect many joints. This includes the knees, ankles, or other joints. A membrane, or protective layer of tissue, surrounds all joints. In JIA, this tissue becomes inflamed. This leads to swelling, pain, and stiffness in certain joints.

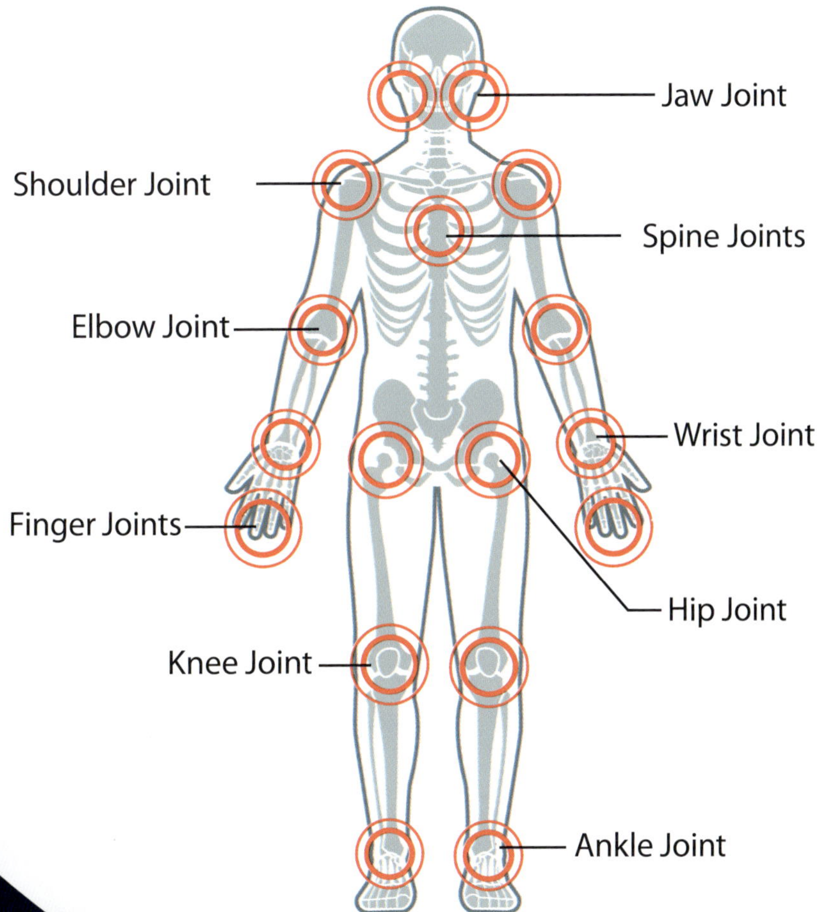

Chapter 1

ELLA'S SOCCER GAME

Eleven-year-old Ella sat and watched her teammates playing soccer. Her best friend stole the ball from the other team. She dodged opposing players and kicked the ball into the net. Ella jumped to her feet and cheered.

Soon, their coach would swap players. Ella would be out on the field. She couldn't wait. She was reminded that, not long ago, she hadn't been able to play soccer. She hadn't been able to play any sports.

Ella had first noticed her joint pain a year ago. She had felt it in her knuckles and wrists. Her fingers hurt as she did her homework. Then it had gotten worse.

◂ **Certain sports, such as soccer, may be challenging for people with JIA.**

TYPES OF JIA

There are different types of JIA. People with systemic JIA have a fever and rashes in addition to the arthritis. Oligoarthritis affects four joints or fewer. Polyarticular arthritis occurs when there is arthritis in five or more joints. A scaly red rash called psoriasis develops in those with psoriatic arthritis. People with enthesitis-related arthritis can have inflammation in their **tendons**, large joints, and sometimes the spine. Types of JIA that do not fit into these categories are called undifferentiated.

Ella noticed stiffness and pain in her jaw, shoulders, back, and hips. One day, the pain got to be so bad that Ella couldn't walk. Her parents took her to doctors, who diagnosed her with JIA. The doctors started her on pills to control the inflammation. Ella had to take pills several times a day.

It was a hard time. The medicines made Ella feel sick. She missed a lot of school. She missed participating in after-school sports.

▲ **Doctors can diagnose and treat people with JIA.**

Ella's doctor later prescribed her medicine in the form of shots. She was given one shot each week. The medicines seemed to work. Ella's joints ached less, and the swelling went down.

Now, Ella was ready to get back in the game. The coach waved her out onto the field. Ella was happy her treatments were working. She was well enough to play sports with her friends again.

Chapter 2

BRETT'S APPOINTMENT

Twelve-year-old Brett looked at his reflection in the wall mirror. He was in a **physical therapy** office, waiting for his appointment. Regular physical therapy helped Brett manage his JIA.

Brett's doctor gave him **steroids** to treat his JIA. The steroids helped control the inflammation in Brett's joints. They also decreased his joint stiffness and swelling. But the steroids had many other effects, including weight gain, rashes, and rapid mood changes. Brett had recently become more aware of the changes in his appearance.

Brett wasn't yet used to the ways the steroids had changed his body. But he was finally feeling better.

◀ Physical therapists can teach people with JIA exercises to help them stay flexible.

▲ **Some sports, such as swimming, can help relieve stiffness and joint pain in people with JIA.**

He was feeling stronger at swim practice now. Swimming helped Brett exercise without putting too much stress on his joints.

Brett practiced an exercise his physical therapist had suggested while he waited for his appointment to start.

He placed his palms on a table. He stretched out his fingers. He counted to 30, then relaxed.

Stretching exercises helped improve Brett's range of motion. It felt good to be able to do something about his joint pain. The exercises helped him relax.

The office door opened. The physical therapist entered. She smiled when she saw him doing his exercises. Brett smiled back.

STAYING FLEXIBLE

Joint pain may cause someone to become less active, which weakens the person's muscles. JIA can also cause scarring around the joints and tendons, which limits motion. Stretching helps joints continue to have the same or improved ranges of motion. Exercises such as stretching against elastic bands called tension bands help build strength. These exercises can also help maintain or improve a person's overall physical condition.

Chapter 3

GOLFER KRISTY McPHERSON

JIA became a part of Kristy McPherson's life when she was 11 years old. On her way home from school one day, her older brother tackled her in their yard. Kristy cried out. She felt a sudden pain in her back. She knew immediately that something was wrong.

Not long after her back started hurting, Kristy noticed a rash on her throat. Her whole body ached. Later, her throat became swollen, making it hard for her to breathe.

Kristy's parents took her to a hospital. Doctors diagnosed her with Still's disease. Today, Still's disease is called systemic JIA. Systemic JIA is a rare form of JIA that affects the whole body. Kristy was unable to walk.

◀ **Kristy McPherson's JIA did not stop her from growing up to play golf professionally.**

Kristy spent months in bed while the doctors tried different treatments.

On the days Kristy was well enough to go to school, her doctors warned her not to play any sports that involved running or jumping. These activities would put too much stress on her joints. But she could participate in activities that weren't hard on her joints, such as golf.

Kristy loved golf. But her school didn't have a girls' golf team. She played with the boys instead. She became a top player on the team. She later earned an athletic scholarship from the University of South Carolina. Then she became a professional golfer. Kristy has played at more than 60 professional golf competitions and won two.

Today, Kristy continues to take medication to control her JIA. She still plays golf. She also works with the Arthritis National Research Foundation. Her work helps young people with JIA find ways to stay active.

Kristy waves to fans at a golf tournament in California in 2009. ▶

TOUR

Chapter 4

ROSA'S TRIP

Twelve-year-old Rosa straightened up from her suitcase, rubbing her elbow. She felt a twinge of pain at the joint. She hoped her JIA wouldn't flare up while she was on her trip. She stretched out her arm for a minute, then got back to packing.

It was hard for Rosa to believe that it had been almost a year since the swelling and inflammation in her joints had started. A year ago, the pain had been so bad that she hadn't been able to dress herself. The pain kept her awake at night. The side effects of her medications, including nausea and vomiting, had made it hard for her to focus. It had been a nightmare. Rosa did not want to go back to that.

◂ **Kids with JIA may struggle with certain tasks, such as packing luggage.**

▲ **Doctors help kids with JIA find the medication that works best for them, which may include shots or pills.**

But after doctors had helped her find the right medicines, Rosa's pain had mostly gone away. The doctors told Rosa that her JIA was in remission.

That meant that her JIA symptoms had temporarily disappeared. Rosa had been relieved, but she knew remission wasn't the same thing as being cured. She still had JIA. Her symptoms might come back again.

Rosa tucked her medication into her suitcase. Then she stopped packing for a moment. She remembered that the hotel had a pool, and swimming helped her manage her JIA. She went to her dresser and pulled out a swimsuit. After adding the suit, Rosa closed the lid on her suitcase and zipped it up. She was ready for her trip.

THINK ABOUT IT

- Have you ever had to do something while you were in pain? How did it affect you?
- Think of your favorite sport or activity. How might you adapt it for someone who has JIA?
- How can you be a good friend to someone who has JIA?

GLOSSARY

diagnose (dye-uhg-NOHS): To diagnose is to identify the disease, disorder, or illness a patient has. JIA symptoms may not develop for a while and may be confused with the flu, which makes the disease hard to diagnose.

genes (JEENZ): Genes are located within the body's cells, and they determine which traits are passed down to a child from the parents. Some scientists think JIA may be caused by a problem in a person's genes.

immune system (i-MYOON SISS-tuhm): The immune system is the part of a person's body that fights against infections and diseases. When someone has JIA, the person's immune system mistakenly attacks healthy cells and tissues.

inflammation (in-fluh-MAY-shuhn): Inflammation is the movement of cells to one part of a person's body, which causes that part of the body to become swollen and painful. People who have JIA have inflammation in the tissues in and around their joints.

physical therapy (FIZ-i-kuhl THAYR-uh-pee): Physical therapy is an exercise-based treatment that helps people recover from injuries, diseases, or disabilities. Brett's physical therapy exercises helped him improve his range of motion.

steroids (STAYR-oidz): Steroids are a type of medicine that can be used to reduce inflammation. Brett took steroids to help control the symptoms of JIA.

tendons (TEN-duhnz): Tendons are strong bands of tissue that connect muscles to bones. Some people with JIA have inflammation in their tendons.

virus (VY-ruhss): A virus is an organism that can cause a disease. Some scientists think that JIA is caused by a virus.

TO LEARN MORE

Books

Bjorklund, Ruth. *Arthritis*. Tarrytown, NY: Marshall Cavendish, 2010.

Gray, Susan H. *The Skeletal System*. Mankato, MN: The Child's World, 2015.

Kenney, Karen Latchana. *Immune System*. Minneapolis, MN: Jump!, 2017.

Web Sites

Visit our Web site for links about juvenile idiopathic arthritis: childsworld.com/links

Note to Parents, Teachers, and Librarians: We routinely verify our Web links to make sure they are safe and active sites. So encourage your readers to check them out!

SELECTED BIBLIOGRAPHY

"Living with JIA." *National Rheumatoid Arthritis Society*. National Rheumatoid Arthritis Society, n.d. Web. 13 Dec. 2017.

Szer, Ilona S. (ed.). *Arthritis in Children and Adolescents: Juvenile Idiopathic Arthritis*. New York, NY: Oxford University Press, 2006.

"What Is Juvenile Arthritis?" *Arthritis National Research Foundation*. Arthritis National Research Foundation, n.d. Web. 13 Dec. 2017.

INDEX

ABOUT THE AUTHOR

James Bow is the author of more than 40 nonfiction books for children. He is a graduate of the University of Waterloo in Ontario, Canada, and a freelance writer and editor. He currently lives outside Toronto, Canada, with his wife and two daughters.